A JOURNEY TO

Victorious Praying

FINDING

DESCIPLINE

AND DELIGHT

IN YOUR

PRAYER LIFE

STUDY GUIDE

Bill Thrasher

MOODY PUBLISHERS
CHICAGO

Contents

*In the end, it is not knowing about
prayer that will change our lives,
but actually doing it.*

— Erwin Lutzer

How to Use this Study Guide

First, we must have a goal: *To become a person of prayer.*

What does that even mean? It means that prayer is a central part of your daily experience. A defining characteristic. It means that you are a person who walks with God, led by the Spirit, abiding in Christ. A person of prayer is following in Christ's steps, going to the Father night and day, in all circumstances and seasons of the heart.

How does one become a person of prayer?

Like any other defining characteristic, it takes perseverance. Though we're describing a relationship, even the best of relationships require effort and investment. That's because relationships draw upon and shape who you are.

As you walk with God in prayer, you learn who He is and what He's like. You come to recognize His ways and desire His will. All the while, whether you know it or not, you are growing in wisdom and influence. Your character is changing as peace, faith, patience, and love take root in your life. And you are gaining strength. You are learning to move men, by God, through prayer.

Kingdom work is not easy work. It requires heavy lifting, involves spiritual engagement, and often comes with strong opposition.

Is becoming a person of prayer worth the investment? There's no question about it! As your life changes, God does His kingdom work among the people you touch, bringing glory to Himself in the process.

Are you ready? He is waiting!

How this study guide works
This booklet is a companion guide to *A Journey to Victorious Praying: Finding Discipline and Delight in Your Prayer Life,* by Bill Thrasher.

Ideal either for individual, one-on-one, or group study, it follows an eight-week format (five days per week). However, you can use it as you deem fit. Sprint through it in a few weeks or mosey along at your own pace. Either way, allow God to guide your journey.

Each page in the study consists of one "day" and references several pages from *A Journey to Victorious Praying* that can be read for context. The opening paragraph for each day summarizes a key concept from those pages, and the questions are designed to help you apply that theme to your prayer life. You'll also find individual Scriptures at the bottom of each page to help you focus your time in prayer.

You may also wish to take advantage of these additional resources:

- A series of video sessions featuring Bill Thrasher teaching this material is available both online and on DVD. For more information, visit www.moodypublishers.com.
- Suggestions for keeping a personal prayer journal can be found on page 225 of *A Journey to Victorious Praying*.
- A list of selected prayers from Scripture can be found on page 233 of the book.
- A list of ideas to stimulate individual or group prayer can be found on page 245 of the book.

The prayer of the upright is a delight to the Lord (Proverbs 15:8).

My hope for this study guide is that it will enable you to experience afresh God's delight in you.

Designed as an eight-week exercise, it can easily be expanded if you choose to take longer on any given week.

It is my joy to pray for the readers of *A Journey to Victorious Praying* each day. May God meet you in a special way as you participate in this study.

— Dr. Bill Thrasher

DAY 1

Transforming Fear into Faith

(Further Reading: Pages 17-21)

❧

Prayer is an attitude of helplessness. This attitude of helplessness is not meant to drive you to anxiety but rather to drive you to God. In other words, prayer is helplessness plus faith. When we petition God in prayer, we come to Christ and tell Him what we, and those for whom we pray, are lacking. It is opening up our needy lives to Him.

Discussion and Discovery:

1. How does the Psalmist respond to his fears? Read Psalm 34:4.

2. How can a person respond to the temptation of anxiety in a way that moves him or her to prayer? Read Philippians 4:6–7.

3. Do you have any specific fears and/or anxieties that can provide motivation for you to pray? Write them down.

4. What is the "Isaac" in your life that you need to surrender to the Lord? See page 21.

Additional Scripture for Prayer:

- 1 Peter 5:7
- 2 Timothy 1:12

DAY 2

Praying with Confidence When You Feel Unworthy

(Further Reading: Pages 23–25)

৵৵৵

We are to come to God in Jesus' name (John 14:14). We must pray for things that are in line with His revealed character and would enhance His reputation. The key is to come to God with confidence during our needy moments. Humble yourself before Him and let Him use your life to display to the world how kind and gracious He is.

Discussion and Discovery:

1. What does it mean to "pray in the name of Jesus"?

2. Write down one area of your life in which you feel inadequate or unworthy. What would it mean to "pray in the name Jesus" about this concern?

3. Look at Ephesians 2:7. What did you learn about the kindness of Jesus' name?

4. Review the activities of your day. Now write down any guidance you receive from 1 Corinthians 10:31 and Colossians 3:17.

Additional Scripture for Prayer:

■ Proverbs 22:1

DAY 3

Sharing Your True Desires with God

(Further Reading: Pages 27-32)

There are many opportunities throughout each day that encourage you to draw near with confidence to God's throne of grace. When you are struggling with anger, you need His merciful and gracious aid. You will receive it only if you first come to God and tell Him about your struggle.

Discussion and Discovery:

1. Review Jim's testimony of God's response to his honesty in prayer (page 27). What are some of your observations?

2. Are there any hurts, pains, or temptations you face for which you need to come boldly to the throne of grace and receive His mercy and grace? Write them down. And come freely.

3. Read Mark 1:40–42. Where can you trust Jesus to put His loving hand on your hurts?

Additional Scripture for Prayer:

■ Hebrews 4:15–16
■ James 4:6

DAY 4

Sharing Your True Desires with God
(Review: Pages 27-32)

☙❧

Temptations are an appeal to meet righteous needs in an unrighteous way. Come to God; thank Him that He has a righteous way to meet the longing your temptation has stirred.

Discussion and Discovery:

1. Look at 1 John 1:7. Write down the meaning of the phrase "walk in the light" as it is explained on page 30.

2. Read 1 John 1:7 again. What is the result of walking in the light? Can you purpose to "walk in the light" with every temptation in your life for the next 24 hours? Or even longer?

3. Ponder Nathan's rebuke to David in 2 Samuel 12:7–14. Use this rebuke as a motivation to tell your deepest desires to the Lord rather than going somewhere else to have your needs met.

4. How is temptation in your life an attempt at meeting a legitimate need in an unrighteous way? Ask God to show you what desires you are trying to fulfill.

Additional Scripture for Prayer:

■ John 6:35

DAY 5

Turning Your Temptations into Victorious Prayer
(Further Reading: Pages 33-38)

☙❧

The key is to ask God what He wants you to pray. It should be the prayer burden that He gives you. As you turn your temptation into meaningful intercession you will find yourself engaging in true prayer.

Discussion and Discovery:

1. Do you believe that God wins His victories in the midst of apparent defeat? Consider the following three examples, then explain:
   - The death and resurrection of Christ
   - Revelation 11:3–13
   - 2 Corinthians 1:8–9

2. Can you list past times of apparent defeat in your life that were precursors to special spiritual opportunities?

3. Read Psalm 27:8. Explain how God is encouraging His people to seek Him in their times of temptation.

4. Ask God to give you a specific prayer burden to pray every time you encounter your most persistent temptation. Write it down.

Additional Scripture for Prayer:

- Genesis 20:17–18
- Luke 18:9–14

DAY 1

Experiencing the Spirit's Motivation in Prayer

(Further Reading: Pages 41-45)

࿇

We must cooperate with the Holy Spirit to develop a fervency and compassion in our prayers. We cannot work this up on our own strength. As all of life is to be lived in dependence on the Holy Spirit, so in our prayer life we are to depend on the Spirit of God for motivation.

Discussion and Discovery:

1. Would you know if your prayer life died? How?

2. What are the five commands in relationship to the Holy Spirit? Read Galatians 5:16; Ephesians 4:30; Ephesians 5:18; 1 Thessalonians 5:19; and Ephesians 6:18 and Jude 20.

3. What is the meaning of the Greek word "Paraclete"?

4. How can you trust God to develop a fervency in your prayer life? Will you ask Him for it?

Additional Scripture for Prayer:

- Isaiah 64:7
- Luke 22:44
- Acts 12:5
- Romans 15:30

DAY 2

Receiving Strength to Believe God

(Further Reading: Pages 47-50)

❧❧

In prayer we are to ask God what He wants us to believe Him for. And we are to concurrently recognize that our faith in this matter is a prime target of the evil one in the spiritual battle of every believer's life.

Discussion and Discovery:

1. Read 1 Thessalonians 3:5. What is the devil's work here that you can observe?

2. Look at Ephesians 6:10 and Romans 4:20. The same Greek word "be strong" is used in both of these passages. Is there a particular area of concern in your life in which you can ask the Lord to strengthen your faith?

3. Review the story of the college student on pages 48–50. What is the Spirit of God empowering you to believe Him for today?

Additional Scripture for Prayer:

■ Ephesians 3:16–17
■ James 4:7
■ Romans 15:5

DAY 3

Being Guided in Prayer

(Further Reading: Pages 51-56)

ಸಾಶ

True prayer starts with God and the prayer burden He places on our heart. For that reason the greatest discipline in prayer is the discipline of communicating with the Holy Spirit as He aids us in sharing our real concerns.

Discussion and Discovery:

1. Begin by asking God how He desires to aid you in being sensitive to His promptings to pray today.

2. Write down the three greatest concerns of your heart and share these with the Lord right now.

3. Look at Psalm 38:9, Psalm 62:8, and Romans 10:1. Write down what each of these verses teach you about prayer.

4. Review the illustrations on pages 54 and 55 again. Do you have any unhealthy addiction to "noise" in your life? Ask God for the grace to free you from it and to make you willing to use the discipline of silence.

Additional Scripture for Prayer:

■ Read Psalm 62:8 one more time. Ask God to really help you believe what it says.

DAY 4

When You Don't Know How to Pray

(Further Reading: Pages 57-60)

࿇

As we lean upon the Spirit's help to give us motivation, enablement, and guidance, there will be times of special weakness. It is in these times that the Holy Spirit lends us a helping hand. The Holy Spirit helps us present the deep desires of our heart to the Father, who graciously answers them.

Discussion and Discovery:

1. Read Romans 8:26–27. What did you learn about prayer from these verses?

2. Read 2 Corinthians 12:7–10. What did you learn about how God chooses to answer prayer from these verses?

3. Is there some longing in your heart that is not being answered? Could it be because God wants to grant you an even deeper longing and desire of your heart?

Additional Scripture for Prayer:

■ 2 Corinthians 12:1–10

16

DAY 5

Receiving the Help of the Holy Spirit

(Review: Pages 41-60)

❧

The Holy Spirit is our gracious Helper in prayer. We need His assistance in all our prayers. We are to look to Him for motivation, to empower us to believe God, and to guide our prayers. Sometimes we must submit to our weakness and in humility allow the Holy Spirit to lay bare our hearts before God.

Discussion and Discovery:

1. Review your answers to the questions of the previous four days. Ask God to breathe new life into your times of prayer.

2. Prepare yourself for the Lord's Day this week by reviewing the three greatest concerns of your heart that you wrote down two days ago. Surrender them again to the Lord, in faith.

3. What have you learned about the Holy Spirit this last week that you didn't know before? How will that change how you pray?

Additional Scripture for Prayer:

■ Read Galatians 5:16–26. How can you live *by the Spirit?*

DAY 1

Receiving Help in Prayer from Others
(Further Reading: Pages 63-67)

∂∽⌐

As we seek to cast our cares upon the Lord, we need to be alert to the times that God wants to use others to aid us. Sometimes we need others to pray with us and for us in order to experience the peace Jesus gives.

Discussion and Discovery:

1. What do Proverbs 27:17 and Ecclesiastes 4:9–12 say in regard to the benefit of companionship?

2. Read Philippians 4:6–7, 1 Peter 5:7, Psalms 55:22, and Galatians 6:2. Are there any burdens you need to give over to God?

3. Of these concerns, are there any that you need to share with others in order to help you bear them up in prayer?

Additional Scripture for Prayer:

■ Matthew 26:37–38
■ John 14:27

DAY 2

Achieving Victories You Never Thought Possible

(Further Reading: Pages 69-73)

❧❧

Whatever your need or crisis may be, it is wise to follow the pattern in Scripture of informing your friends about it and requesting the compassion of our wonderful God in prayer.

Discussion and Discovery:

1. Read Daniel 2:17–18 and Acts 4:23-24. What principle of prayer do you glean from these verses?

2. Pray through the three suggestions on page 72. Discuss these options and a few possible courses of action with someone you trust.

3. Is God prompting you to request prayer for any specific issue in your life? Explain.

Additional Scripture for Prayer:

■ Read Acts 4:23–31

DAY 3

Learning When to Fast

(Further Reading: Pages 141-147)

෮ඁ

There is nothing meritorious to fasting, in the sense that one earns favor from God. Every spiritual discipline should rest on the foundation of Christ's already finished work. However, fasting as a discipline can help us to experience the life of victory that Christ has purchased for us.

Discussion and Discovery:

1. How does Richard Foster define fasting (page 143)? Does that seem like something you want to do?

2. What is the purpose of fasting according to O. Hallesby (page 143)? Do you agree?

3. Read Ephesians 1:3. How does this verse guard one against viewing fasting as a way to earn God's blessings?

4. What are some different kinds of fasts (pages 144–145)?

5. When should we fast (pages 145–147)?

Additional Scripture for Prayer:

- Matthew 9:15
- Acts 14:23

DAY 4

Experiencing the Benefits of Fasting

(Further Reading: Pages 149-156)

⤞⤝

The aim of fasting is to cultivate a conscious enjoyment of God's presence in one's life. If you desire true contentment and joy in God, then you will find the discipline of fasting helpful, as it strengthens the intensity of your prayers and your repentance.

Discussion and Discovery:

1. What did you learn from the story of the Church of the Foothills (pages 149–154)? Is any of it applicable to your life?

2. What are some of the physical benefits of fasting?

3. Write down what you see as the most significant spiritual benefit of fasting.

Additional Scripture for Prayer:

■ Luke 2:37
■ Joel 2:12
■ John 15:5

DAY 5

Getting Started

(Further Reading: Pages 157-160)

༈

We should fast as God directs and empowers us. We do not live under any command that prescribes when or how often we are to fast. Often the obstacle that prevents someone from fasting is fear—so we ought to first prepare by confessing and repenting of any such fears.

Discussion and Discovery:

1. What are four abuses of the discipline of fasting (pages 157–158)?

2. What spiritual purpose is God giving you to motivate a fast?

3. If you feel the Spirit's leading and direction, plan a fast of dedication to express your willingness to fast.

4. In what areas of your life might a fast yield an unburdening from the things of this world?

Additional Scripture for Prayer:

- Joel 2:15–16
- 1 Corinthians 9:24–27
- Nehemiah 1:4

DAY 1

Learning George Mueller's Secret

(Further Reading: Pages 77-81)

☞∽✦

George Mueller prayed that his life and work would display convincing proof that God hears prayer and that it is always safe to trust Him. Mueller centered his life around prayer and Scripture intake—he took both very seriously.

Discussion and Discovery:

1. Look at George Mueller's life purpose and ask God to give you a purpose that will clearly honor Him. If you already know His answer to you, write it down.

2. What hindered Mueller's devotion to Scripture in the early years of his Christian life?

3. What obstacles in your life keep you from finding time to get into God's Word? Write them down and believe God to overcome them.

4. What main principle can be gained from Romans 10:17?

Additional Scripture for Prayer:

■ Joshua 1:8–9
■ Psalm 1:2–3
■ James 1:25

DAY 2

Experiencing True Prosperity
(Further Reading: Pages 83-88)

෧෨

In meditation we see a vital link between the discipline of Scripture reading and the discipline of prayer. Without prayer the study of Scripture can turn into a merely intellectual exercise. Without Scripture the practice of prayer can lack motivation and guidance.

Discussion and Discovery:

1. Re-read the definition of "meditation" on page 84. Is this how you have understood meditation in the past?

2. Read John 15:7. What two seemingly separate disciplines are connected in this passage?

3. Ask God to open up some familiar Scriptures to you. Ask Him to explain Psalm 37:4 and Galatians 5:16. This is meditating. Be patient but expectant. Scripture fuels the fire of your prayer life.

Additional Scripture for Prayer:

Pray with your unsaved friends in mind . . .
- Matthew 9:38
- Colossians 4:3
- Ephesians 6:19–20

DAY 3

Experiencing True Prosperity

(Further Reading: Pages 83-88)

When we come to the point of realizing our weakness in prayer, we begin to make progress. It is our weakness that not only draws us to the Lord, causing us to depend on the Holy Spirit in prayer, but also compels us to read God's Word to learn how to express our hearts in prayer.

Discussion and Discovery:

1. Read Psalm 17 and Psalm 86. What do these chapters tell you about prayer?

2. Do any other Psalms come to mind that remind you to rely on God's wisdom rather than your own?

3. Write down some requests that the Psalms encourage you to pray.

Additional Scripture for Prayer:

- 2 Samuel 7:27

DAY 4

Learning How to Pray for Christ-like Growth

(Further Reading: Pages 89-94)

৵৹৵

Knowing Christ is the greatest joy in life. He alone can strengthen our spirits, give us His wisdom, and supply us His grace. We ought to let our inadequacy draw us to God and believe that He will answer the requests of our hearts, as they pull us closer to His heart.

Discussion and Discovery:

1. Read Luke 2:40. Pray the three requests from this verse on behalf of a loved one.

2. Read Ephesians 3:14–21. Why is praying for inward strength valuable?

3. Read James 1:5 and Colossians 1:9–12. Should we pray for wisdom? How?

4. Read Hebrews 4:16 and 1 Corinthians 15:10. What is grace? Is it something we should approach God for?

Additional Scripture for Prayer:

- Luke 2:40–52
- Romans 8:9
- Proverbs 17:21, 25
- 2 Corinthians 12:7–10

DAY 5

Learning to Pray Scripture

(Further Reading: Pages 95-102)

જજ

The first step in effectively using a scriptural prayer is to understand it. The second step is to pray it. If you seek only to understand a scriptural prayer without bringing it before God, then you are ignoring that part of God's Word.

Discussion and Discovery:

1. Write down the requests of Ephesians 1:15–23. Then pray this scriptural prayer.

2. Write down the requests of Ephesians 3:14–21. Then pray this scriptural prayer.

3. Write down the requests of Philippians 1:9–11. Then pray this scriptural prayer.

4. Write down the requests of Colossians 1:9–12. Then pray this scriptural prayer.

Additional Scripture for Prayer:

■ Ephesians 1:3–14
■ Isaiah 9:6
■ Proverbs 7:1
■ 1 John 5:14–15

DAY 1

Realizing the Struggle of Prayer

(Further Reading: Pages 105-109)

❧

Let's be honest: Most of us are overextended. Too often, we fail to grasp that if our Christian service does not flow from an abiding relationship with Christ, then it is the fruit of our flesh rather than the Spirit.

Discussion and Discovery:

1. Read 2 Corinthians 11:3. What is the scheme of the devil in this verse? How does he use it against you?

2. Read the illustration on pages 105 and 106 again. Write down how you are tempted to keep busy with the non-essentials of life and neglect prayer.

3. Write down a prayer response to Hudson Taylor's words, "As wounds when healed often leave a scar, so the sin of neglected communion may be forgiven, and yet the effect remains permanently."

Additional Scripture for Prayer:

■ Deuteronomy 10:13
■ John 10:10

DAY 2

Realizing the Struggle of Prayer
(Review: Pages 105-109)

ভ∽ঔ

Cultivating meaningful disciplines in our lives is a struggle. Yet if a Christian has never known spiritual struggles, there is likely to be a lack of depth in that person's development.

Discussion and Discovery:

1. Read Deuteronomy 10:13. What is the purpose of God's commandments according to this passage?

2. Read Colossians 4:2. What instructions can you glean?

3. Read Daniel 6:10 and Acts 6:4. What do you learn from these passages about the discipline of prayer?

4. Describe your struggle with the discipline of prayer. What was Richard Baxter's solution on pages 107-109?

Additional Scripture for Prayer:

■ Colossians 4:2

DAY 3

Understanding Jesus' Patterns of Prayer

(Further Reading: Pages 111-118)

જ્જઠ

There is more at stake in prayer than we know. Therefore, we must go to the Master to observe His example. When did Jesus pray? Certainly He modeled a lifestyle of prayer, but we also can observe definite times and patterns of prayer in His life and ministry. Let's look at some of them.

Discussion and Discovery:

1. Read Luke 6:12–13. What principle stands out most to you from this passage?

2. Read Matthew 14:22–23. What principle stands out most to you from this passage?

3. Read Mark 1:35. What principle stands out most to you from this passage?

4. Read pages 114 and 115 again. What is the difference between spending time with God and investing time with Him?

Additional Scripture for Prayer:

■ Read Luke 6, Matthew 14, and Mark 1, paying special attention to the circumstances and contexts that led Jesus to intense times of prayer.

DAY 4

More on Jesus' Patterns of Prayer
(Review: Pages 111-118)

෬෧

Our goal is to develop a healthy lifestyle of prayer in which we continually share our hearts with God. This practice will, of course, look different for every believer in terms of habits and forms. But this lifestyle of prayer must be our priority.

Discussion and Discovery:

1. Read Isaiah 50:4–5 carefully. What principle of ministry can be gleaned from the prophetic picture in this passage of Jesus' devotional life?

2. Read Matthew 9:35–38. What principle stands out most to you from this passage?

3. What do you learn from Stonewall Jackson's quote on page 118 that might have applicability in your everyday life?

Additional Scripture for Prayer:

■ Read Matthew 9, again noting the circumstances and contexts that surrounded Jesus' intense times of prayer.

ᵭAY 5

Realizing the Struggle of Prayer
(Review: Pages 105-118)

かへふ

It is Jesus Christ's sacrificial death alone that has purchased for us every spiritual blessing. In the discipline of prayer we put ourselves in position to receive what He has already graciously provided. Why? Because He has chosen to work through prayer. In prayer your very life can bring great delight to God.

Discussion and Discovery:

1. Everything you have been learning thus far is related. Write down how you would advise someone to enrich their discipline of prayer (this section) using the previous sections of the book.

   ■ The Help of Their Weakness:

   ■ The Help of the Holy Spirit:

   ■ The Help of Companionship and Fasting:

   ■ The Help of Scripture:

Additional Scripture for Prayer:

■ Ephesians 1:3
■ Proverbs 15:8

DAY 1

Gaining Strength Through Prayer
(Further Reading: Pages 121-124)

⌒⌒

Should an occasional jogger despair after watching an Olympic marathon because he cannot match the athletes' performance? Certainly not! It would be equally unwise to despair rather than be instructed, encouraged, and challenged by those who have been taught of God.

Discussion and Discovery:

1. Review the commitment of George McCluskey (pages 121–122) and write down your thoughts and a response you will take.

2. Do you agree with the "4 Keys to Discipleship" on pages 122–123? Explain.

Additional Scripture for Prayer:

■ Think through the stories of some favorite Bible characters. What role did prayer play in their lives?

DAY 2

Realizing God's Desire to Bless You

(Further Reading: Pages 125-129)

૭∽ళ

The most effective way to communicate the nature and importance of true prayer is to realize that it all begins with an understanding of God. It is God Himself who gave us His inspired revelation to teach us the utmost importance of prayer.

Discussion and Discovery:

1. Read Matthew 7:7–11. Write down everything you learn about prayer from this passage.

2. What is the difference between viewing God through the lens of your guilty conscience and viewing Him through the lens of Christ?

3. Do you see God as good toward you? The first step is realizing that you have earned His wrath. Yet in His mercy, Christ has earned for you every spiritual blessing. The second step is humbling yourself before God and receiving His goodness and grace.

Additional Scripture for Prayer:

- 1 Thessalonians 5:17
- Deuteronomy 10:13
- 1 Samuel 12:23

DAY 3

Realizing God's Desire to Bless You

(Review: Pages 125-129)

❧

If we insist on having our own way, God will give it to us. He encourages
His redeemed people to open their mouths and let Him graciously fill
them. If His people refuse to listen to Him, He will give them over "to the
stubbornness of their heart" (Psalm 81:12).

Discussion and Discovery:

1. Write down the gifts that can be received through prayer in each one
of the following verses:

■ Romans 10:13

■ Philippians 4:6–7

■ John 16:24

■ 2 Chronicles 7:14

■ Luke 18:1

Additional Scripture for Prayer:

■ Isaiah 28:21
■ Luke 6:35

DAY 4

Understanding How God Works

(Further Reading: Pages 131-138)

ôœ

"There is no wonder more supernatural and divine in the life of a believer than the mystery and the ministry of prayer . . . the hand of the child touching the arm of the Father and moving the wheel of the universe."

— A. B. Simpson

Discussion and Discovery:

1. How does God often accomplish His work (page 131)?

2. Read Isaiah 62:6–7. What does this passage teach about God's method of working?

3. Read 1 Timothy 2:1–2. What is the first priority of the gathered church according to these verses?

4. Read Matthew 9:35–38. What do these verses reveal about God's method of getting His work done?

Additional Scripture for Prayer:

■ Read the quote from Andrew Murray on page 134 one more time. Then re-read the above verses.

DAY 5

Realizing God's Desire to Bless You
(Further Reading: Pages 125-129)

❧

One of the wisest requests you can make is: "Lord, teach me to pray."

Discussion and Discovery:

1. Begin this review section by earnestly asking God to teach your heart the importance of prayer.

2. Has God laid any new (or old) prayer burdens on your heart today? Explain.

3. Remember that prayer begins with God, and He will enable you to pray the burdens that He puts on your heart as you humble yourself before Him. List your primary burdens and discuss them with God.

Additional Scripture for Prayer:

■ Proverbs 15:8

DAY 1

Experiencing the Joy of Waiting

(Further Reading: Pages 163-168)

অ৽৵

Abiding in the Lord and waiting on Him is the only way to live a life of eternal significance. As we abide in the Lord we can do an eternal work even in the midst of the routines of life. We are able to accomplish nothing of eternal value apart from the enablement of Christ (John 15:5).

Discussion and Discovery:

1. Read Luke 10:38–42. Why does Jesus rebuke Martha and commend Mary (see pages 165-167)?

2. What are some of the benefits of waiting on God?

- Psalm 25:3

- Psalm 37:9

- Psalm 147:11

- Isaiah 40:31

- Isaiah 64:4

- Lamentations 3:26

Additional Scripture for Prayer:

- Isaiah 30:15

DAY 2

Discovering God's Purposes While You Wait

(Further Reading: Pages 169-175)

ॐ∽

We are to come to God as His servant and not as His master. The essence of prayer is found in the Lord's words in Gethsemane, "Yet not what I will, but what You will" (Mark 14:36). If one prays to God in a spirit that refuses to listen to God's Word, that prayer is said to be an abomination (Proverbs 28:9).

Discussion and Discovery:

1. Read John 15:7 and pages 169 to 170. How would you explain this verse to John, Tom, and Dorothy's friends who have experienced great disappointments in their prayers?

2. Read James 4:7 and pages 171–172. What does it mean to "submit to God"?

3. What is your understanding of D. L. Moody's quote: "Very often when we cry to God, we do not really mean anything"?

Additional Scripture for Prayer:

- Mark 14:36
- Proverbs 28:9
- James 4:2–3

DAY 3

Discovering God's Purposes While You Wait

(Further Reading: Pages 169-175)

❧❦

A great emphasis in prayer is what God desires to do in us. He wants to get us under His loving authority, dependent on His Spirit, walking in the Light, motivated by His love, and living for His glory. The essence of these five truths is an abandonment of one's life to the Lord and a continual openness, dependence, and responsiveness to His loving control.

Discussion and Discovery:

1. Re-read the five purposes of God in prayer found in this chapter. What is your greatest concern? Which of God's purposes do you have the hardest time with in your prayer life?

2. What do the following verses teach about prayer?

   ■ Ezekiel 14:3

   ■ Psalm 66:18

   ■ Matthew 5:23–24

   ■ 1 Peter 3:7

   ■ Matthew 6:5

Additional Scripture for Prayer:

■ Mark 11:25
■ Psalm 115:1

DAY 4

Transforming Your Anxiety into Peace

(Further Reading: Pages 177-185)

Concern + Unbelief = Anxiety
Concern + Faith = A Biblical Virtue

Discussion and Discovery:

1. What is the difference between a godly concern and a sinful anxiety?

2. What do the following verses teach about the fruit of anxiety?

- Matthew 6:27

- Mark 4:19

- Luke 21:34

- Luke 10:38–42

3. What do these verses teach about experiencing God's peace?

- Matthew 6:33–34

- Philippians 4:6–7

- Galatians 6:2

Additional Scripture for Prayer:

- 2 Thessalonians 3:16

DAY 5

Knowing When to Keep Praying
(Further Reading: Pages 187-195)

❧

A persevering intercessor is characterized by the ability to see and internal-
ize how God desires to bless another. He or she is also an advocate for the
one who stands in need of this blessing. The most telling trait of such an
intercessor is their faithfulness in pursuing the matter in prayer until it is
received.

Discussion and Discovery:

1. Read Matthew 15:21–28. What does this verse teach about perseverance in your prayers to the Lord?

2. Has God given you any prayer burdens under which you need to persevere? (Seek to use the seven aids to intercession found on page 194.)

3. What benefits have you experienced as you have persevered in prayer?

4. Re-read pages 192–193. Evaluate your prayer requests by the three
   truths under the heading "When should we persevere in prayer?"

Additional Scripture for Prayer:

■ Isaiah 62:6–7
■ Matthew 7:7–11
■ Luke 11:5–8; 18:1–8
■ Genesis 18:22–23; 32:24–29

DAY 1

Experiencing the Goodness of Praise

(Further Reading: Pages 199-206)

രം

If you were perfect in every way, the greatest gift you could give someone would be to allow him or her to enjoy you for who you are. God in His perfection gives to us this gift, and with it come countless other benefits.

Discussion and Discovery:

1. Read John 4:23. What principle do you glean from this passage?

2. Read Psalm 115:4–8. What principle do you glean from this passage?

3. Read page 202. Why does worship strengthen our faith?

Additional Scripture for Prayer:

- 2 Corinthians 3:18
- Daniel 4:34
- Psalm 34:3
- Romans 15:6
- Psalm 22:3
- Psalm 73:17
- Acts 13:2

DAY 2

Understanding the Meaning of True Worship
ᐁᐁ

(Further Reading: Pages 207-212)

The simplest way to define worship is that it attributes worth to God's revealed character. It means that we acknowledge Him for who He is and in this way glorify or honor Him.

Discussion and Discovery:

1. Read Psalm 29:2. Explain its meaning in the context of this chapter.

2. Read William Temple's definition of worship on page 209. Now write down your own definition.

3. Read pages 209 and 210. According to these pages, what is the meaning of the word "heart" in the Scriptures?

4. Now read Henry Blackaby's definition of genuine worship on page 210. What insights do you gain?

Additional Scripture for Prayer:

- Psalm 103:1
- 2 Chronicles 16:9
- Psalm 86:11

DAY 3

Understanding the Meaning of True Worship
(Review: Pages 207-212)

If you are wondering, "How can I cultivate a lifestyle of worship?" then you are asking the most important question that can be asked. There has never been a person who asked this with sincerity, sought God for the answer, and purposed to do anything God would suggest who did not receive an answer.

Discussion and Discovery:

1. What do you learn about thanksgiving and praise from the following verses?

- Psalm 34:1

- Psalm 57:7

- 1 Corinthians 10:31

- 1 Thessalonians 5:18

- Romans 12:1–2

- Philippians 4:16

- Hebrews 13:15–16

Additional Scripture for Prayer:

- Psalm 145:2
- Hebrews 3:17–18

DAY 4

Abiding in the Lord

(Further Reading: Pages 213-218)

ষ্৹ঔ

As you walk openly, honestly, and transparently before God, then and only then will prayer and worship become a dynamic reality in your life. Walking openly and honestly is not to be equated with an absence of struggle. It is rather taking our struggles into the presence of God.

Discussion and Discovery:

1. What does it mean to be open to the Spirit's control? Are you?

2. What does it mean to be dependent upon the Spirit's control? Are you?

3. What does it mean to be responsive to the Spirit's control? Are you?

4. Re-read page 215. What does it mean to activate your faith before you activate your will?

5. What does the filling of the Spirit (Ephesians 5:18) result in, according to Ephesians 5:19–20?

Additional Scripture for Prayer:

■ Psalm 37:5
■ Romans 8:9

DAY 5

Cultivating a Lifestyle of Worship

(Further Reading: Pages 219-223)

ॐ

Worship and praise have great consequence, so do not get discouraged if you experience spiritual opposition. "Greater is He who is in you than he who is in the world" (1 John 4:4). Trust God's wisdom, strength, and love as you seek to make prayer and praise your greatest priority.

Discussion and Discovery:

1. What principle do you learn from Simeon's example in Luke 2:25–35?

2. Meditate on Ephesians 5:20 this entire day. Write down your thoughts.

3. Take some extra time to go through these passages and praise God for the blessings you have in Christ. Write some of these blessings down.

- Romans 5:1–11

- Romans 6:1–23

- Romans 8:1–39

Additional Scripture for Prayer:

- 2 Corinthians 9:12
- James 1:17

www.moodypublishers.com